Naming the Stars

Books by Joyce Sutphen

Naming the Stars (2004)
Coming Back to the Body (2000)
Straight Out of View (1995, 2001)

Naming the Stars

Poems by
Joyce Sutphen

HOLY COW! PRESS · DULUTH, MINNESOTA

Library of Congress Cataloging-in-Publication Data

Sutphen, Joyce
Naming the stars : poems / by Joyce Sutphen.
p. cm.
ISBN 0-930100-05-0 (alk. paper)
1. Interpersonal relations—Poetry. 2. Friendship—Poetry. I. Title
PS3569.U857N36 2004
811'.54—dc21   2003051082

Publisher's Address:
Holy Cow! Press
Post Office Box 3170
Mount Royal Station
Duluth, Minnesota 55803

This project is supported, in part, by a grant from the Outagamie Charitable
Foundation and by donations from generous individuals.

Holy Cow! Press titles are distributed to the trade by Consortium Book Sales
& Distribution, 1045 Westgate Drive, Saint Paul, Minnesota 55114. For
inquiries, please write us and visit our website: www.holycowpress.org.

For You

CONTENTS

I

Naming the Stars   11
Raku Songs   12
Gone Missing   16
To Take Her Home   18
She Doesn't Tell   19
How We Ended Up Together   20
The Unreliable Narrator   21
Learning By Heart   22
The Problem Was   23

II

Handprint   27
One of Those Stories   28
Since You Will Not Send Me Word   29
Remembering Love, Pure and Useless   30
Crossing the Seine at Pont Neuf   31
The Collector's Edition   32
Losing Touch   33
Off Line   34
Hanging Up   35
Polaroid # 2   36
Measuring the Distance   37
Road Talk   38
Notice   39
Ever After   40

III

Alone   43
The Bottom Line   44
The Sound of No One Calling   45

Aisle and View   46
One Afternoon in Early Autumn   48
The Apostate's Creed   49
Empty   50
The Old Enmity   51
Reasons for Leaving   52
What Comes After   53
Advice and Content   54
In the Wake   55
Seeing, Up Close Again   56
The Lamp in the Spine   57
Café Song   58

IV

Riding On Faith   61
This Body   62
Beginning Again   63
What the Elders Taught Us   64
The Future Archaic   65
Walking in Early June   66
Soundings   67
In the Middle of Things   68
After, Always After   69
Now That Anything Could Happen   70
Leaving Friday Harbour   71
What to Pack   72
Getting the Machine   73
Some Glad Morning   74
At the Moment   75
Now, Finally, A Love Song   76

About the Author   77
Acknowledgments   78

NAMING THE STARS

This present tragedy will eventually
turn into myth, and in the mist
of that later telling the bell tolling
now will be a symbol, or, at least,
a sign of something long since lost.

This will be another one of those
loose changes, the rearrangement of
hearts, just parts of old lives
patched together, gathered into
a dim constellation, small consolation.

Look, we will say, you can almost see
the outline there: her fingertips
touching his, the faint fusion
of two bodies breaking into light.

RAKU SONGS

I

He never dated them, but he put what
part of the week it was and gave the time
of day—as in "Thursday, early evening,"
or "Friday, morning," so that when
she read them again how much easier
it was to think that then could be now
and what he said might still be true.

Of the weather, he always had something
to say. Once, in early spring when
the ice melted and then froze again,
he walked on a pond and watched
mud and water ooze under his feet
until the soft ice broke. It was shallow
there, he said, and barely covered his shoes.

II

Intended: one letter,
written in the sun
of the marina, palm trees
and parrots (yellow and green)
squawking overhead
while he watched

sails filling in the breeze,
sending her his letter,
which would cover her
with a fine tropic mist.

Instead: something
he wrote as he
looked out the window
at sparrows
pecking in the dirt.

III

He begins in the kitchen,
but ends up in the library.
First it was a drink, calling
him in, then the need for nuts and bolts.
When he thinks about writing, he sees
pages and pages ahead, scenes moving
by like liquid wallpaper. He dips
his pen in and sends her a small cup.

On the back of the page, he daydreams
in fine-lined designs: spaceships
circling in silent concentration, avoiding
touch, no possibility of collision up there.
Momentum evades me, he says, and then:
No, I evade *it*, until time is short.

IV

Monday—no, Tuesday—this one begins.
He's writing on cream-colored cards,
small ones, no real paper to be found,
but he has a new pen.

With his new pen, he says he loves
her; he imagines walking with her when
she is walking in silence and wonders
what she will say when she begins to speak.

When he walks the neighbor's dog, they both
miss her, he says, and then he comes to the end
of the cards, writes "Good-bye for a while"
and "Love," in tiny letters above his name.

V

He tells her that each word is
surrounded by others that don't
get written. I should be putting down
colors instead, he says, or stoking up
fires, in five different shades. Against
her wishes, he sends a present:
a bird guide, slightly used. Imagine me
paging through it in a school van.
The letter, this time, is on parchment
and crinkles when she folds it,
but the pages of the book are soft

as that bird who unrolled his feathers
and rowed him softly home, or butterflies.
He knew she would see him in it
and know he saw her seeing him in
every word he wrote, every bird she saw.

GONE MISSING

When he says, "See you tomorrow,"
it doesn't always
          mean he will.
Maybe you won't see him for years,
and his name will rust
like a bicycle on a green hillside.

Or, it could be you who disappears,
          like Abbie Hoffman
          or Bernadette Devlin,
to live an entirely
unrecognizable life
          in which you join the PTA
and drive an SUV.

In the summer, you sip iced tea
at the edge of a lake,
watching human beings you love
          slip
          in and out
of the shimmering waters,
returning miraculously time after time.

In winter, you forget the colors
of flowers and the way the path felt
beneath your feet. You think:
he could have fallen off the mountain,

a trail of blue nylon ropes
     dangling
     like an unfinished sentence
     down the page
of whatever day
     he did not return.

TO TAKE HER HOME

Later, on the highway home, when she is
passing everything in sight, she looks
into the rearview mirror, expecting
a squad car, maybe, or a monster truck,

but there is nothing there, except the lights
of cars that are fading in the distance,
and now, there is nothing up ahead. Night
parts its dark waters down to the instant

when she is free—as wind, as speed, as this
song that she summons up again with just
the push of a button, and then the voice
riding the guitar and harmonica.

Whatever hard rain is going to fall
she knows—she's already heard it all.

SHE DOESN'T TELL

When she gets the chance to say what
happened, she doesn't say. She talks
about other people and their
troubles; she never mentions names.

I know she'd expect much more
from anybody else. She'd say:
"Now that's a generic statement.
Tell me something specific please!"

I want to know what she thinks he
thought he was doing when he walked
out of her life, and even more:
I want to know just how she felt.

She isn't going to tell, that much
I can tell, but I wonder why—
doesn't she know we want to know
her? After all this time, we do.

HOW WE ENDED UP TOGETHER

He was good in an emergency, calm
in the middle of a storm. Accidents
didn't surprise him; he was always

ready for whatever came along. You
could count on him; you could make
a deal and he would keep it, even if you

couldn't. His deals were impossible;
his deals were meant to make you fail,
and failing you found yourself in some

sort of emergency, someplace you didn't
want to be, and he was good at getting
you back to the ground, back to your feet.

I chose him for what he could not give me,
and he chose me because I would not ask
until I was desperate and only he could help.

THE UNRELIABLE NARRATOR

Imagine she is you,
and you can't seem to get
anything right.

Your reader is convinced
that you are guilty
of crimes so numerous

he can't begin
to list them. He claims
to be the victim,

which is odd,
since he always
seems untouched.

Imagine, when you try
to say how it has
always seemed that he

is a door locked against
you, a sentry at the gate,
a judge ruling on his bench,

he says, "I suppose you
might tell it that way; you
might even believe that it was true."

LEARNING BY HEART

I began to forget him as I wrote, erasing
every word he said with a long wave of
ink that drowned the sound of his voice
and washed away all traces
of his hands.

It was as if I was wrapping him up in a word
and sending the package somewhere far away,
as if I was losing claim to his heart
the minute I began to say
what he meant to me.

So, of course, I stopped and began to put the words
back into my heart where they belonged,
taking up each letter carefully,
wiping away the tarnish of ink
on the sheen of sound.

Afterwards, pasting in the torn pages, recovering
as much as possible, I read it over
again and again the way one does,
realizing, then, the sad
necessity of rote.

THE PROBLEM WAS

The problem was a different sense of form.
He was all couplets, heroic and closed;
I always wanted to carry on, one line
into the next, never reaching an end,
or, if I did, imagining it might be
the possible beginning to a different train
of thought, which might lead to the exact
opposite of what I was saying now.

The problem was we rhymed in various ways:
he liked perfection; I preferred the wise
conjunction of nearly alike, almost
a match made in heaven, both of us most
certain we knew where to take the next line.
He loved his words the best, and I loved mine.

HANDPRINT

You put your hand up to mine
(to show how well we fit together)

and then you traced the print
upon the page and placed your words

in, around, and between your fingers
(your roving thoughts). That's

when you told me how you would
hold me next time we met. America—

oh, I was that to you, and you were
all states and realms (a little world)

to me. You meant well I know,
even though our love was like the grain

of wheat that fell on rocky ground
(all stone) and each of us alone and far

away from touch of skin and sun, our
palmer's palms, once joined together,

moving like mimes along the thick
invisible years that came between us.

ONE OF THOSE STORIES

Younger, I wasn't tender enough to
listen for the moment of surrender;
I wasn't light enough to be carried
away on a word, wasn't quiet enough
to hear the twig of ordinary conversation
snap underfoot.
            Love arrived unbidden
on my doorstep, and I invited him
in (or course). You would have done much
the same, I think, and made the same mistake.
You would have assumed (as I did) that he
was looking for you when,
                    in fact, he was
simply hoping for a cup of coffee,
wondering how you looked in the morning,
and (yes really) just in the neighborhood.

SINCE YOU WILL NOT SEND ME WORD

Since you will not send me word
I will try to imagine
what you might have said.

I will believe there is a world
where you love me again,
I will talk sweetly.

Since you will not take my hand,
(my hand that was just your
size), I will wave

good-bye again and again.
I will weep bitter tears, and
you shall know you are missed.

Since you will not love me love,
oh secret darling of my heart,
I will fall away

and rock myself to sleep.
I will sing a song
and rock myself to sleep.

REMEMBERING LOVE, PURE AND USELESS

Often, I have returned to the places
we loved. I've walked across that
corner of lawn in Holland Park,

and I've crossed the Hungerford Bridge
and sat at the polished-wood table with
the same menu, impossible to read.

Silence, after however many years—
it is not right, as if the body did not
know the dance, as if chestnut trees
had forgotten they were leaf and blossom,
as if we needed a use for anything.

CROSSING THE SEINE AT PONT NEUF

In Paris, we are already old in love
and quarrel in the epicerie after
the Place du Concorde, our heads
filled with executions and traffic.

The sky over the Left Bank is
turquoise, pink, and gold, and
there is our very own Eiffel Tower!
At the bottom of the Champs Élysées

you list the sorrows of the day,
the little time left to us in Paris,
the years back in the States,
the tiny script of our lives.

You are all for making plans and
have folded and unfolded maps all
afternoon, but even so we missed
our turning and walked the winding

streets for hours. When we are
lost, then I am happy; when we
least expect it, the world comes
flowing back to us like this river.

THE COLLECTOR'S EDITION

Now you are no longer as rare
as a book that no one's ever read,
or sightings of a magical creature
who is, by turn, a fish, a bird, or bear.

I liked you best when no one knew how good
you were, before you were discovered, when
you were just you and I was me and we
didn't have to share us with anyone—but

now that you are no longer rare, I think
I'll buy a case of you and put it by for
another day. Now that you are famous,
I want you to sign this page, carefully.

LOSING TOUCH

As if I had died, you heard nothing
from me after that day, and if you thought
about me at times I never knew.

We went on living our missing lives
as if there were centuries between us.
We could have been on different planets,

except that we weren't, and it was
the same moon (more or less) rising over
(more or less) the same world.

The news happened, and we heard it
together, watching identical faces in
different rooms. Once or twice we probably

passed each other on the freeway or
in the airport. There was a moment of hesitation
before we went on, as if someone had died.

OFF LINE

When you answer the phone, it isn't you
who answers but your voice, and that is why
I write these words that aren't me—simply to
let you know that somewhere in the world I

exist. The tape that you made for me is
playing as I write, telling me what you
would like me to know in someone else's
words. I'd like to send a photograph to

the moon to show her how you look from here;
I'd like to listen so carefully that you
would think you were looking in the mirror
and talking to yourself. I'd say: how do

we get past the memory of who we
are? Who was I when you didn't know me?

HANGING UP

I put the phone back into its cradle.
The world is still for a moment, heavy
as a stone dropping down into a well.

I wish that you cared enough to call me
back, though I can't say what it is I would
want you to say if you did. I love you

then I say to the empty air, and you
say nothing in return. This must be how
it is when the rains do not come in Spring
and the fields can do nothing to bring them
down, or perhaps this is how it is when
the leaves turn yellow and fall from the tree.

I try to be as quiet as the grass,
clear as the empty branch against the sky.

POLAROID #2

You took this picture of me;
because of that I can see how
I once looked to you.

You stood with the lake
behind you and put a frame
around me. Smile, you said.

I can't remember how it felt
to look the way I do
in the picture, but I can

remember how it felt to look
out from that body to where
you stood, telling me to smile.

I'm always smiling in this picture,
but no matter how hard I look,
I can't see to where you're standing,

watching this picture of me come
out of the darkness, holding
the moment in your hand.

MEASURING THE DISTANCE

I am always hungry now.
Ever since the day you left,
nothing fills me up.

At night, I listen for trains
that come along the lake and hear,
like hinges in the wind, the birds.

I never knew the world was so
taken up with the sound of distance,
or that what was near would

sound like seeds cracking
open, skin against skin.
The sky is an old clock now,

each tick talking, a star,
falling slowly out of time.

ROAD TALK

When I tried to explain you
on the way to Cork,
I couldn't get you right.

If I said you were one way,
I remembered you the other,
and the green hills rolled on.

At last, after I'd said some things
I regretted (but only because
they weren't exactly you)

I promised I'd say just one last thing,
"and I don't know why
I'm bothering with that."

"To begin with," I began and
went straight to the very end,
and the green hills rolled on.

NOTICE

Notice how you show up here and there among
the words I use, that there are small details

that only you would notice, especially when you
notice that I am saying things that I never

said before. And see how easy it is to hear
them now that I am not speaking directly

to you, now that you could be anyone who
happened to read these words, and notice how what

I am saying makes you think of things you
haven't noticed in a long time. Notice how

just when you are thinking that it has to be
you I'm talking to, you notice something in

the story that doesn't fit, something that makes you
doubt that you are the you I was talking to.

Then notice how you are turning away from
me again the way I always say you do.

EVER AFTER

What am I to you now that you are no
longer what you used to be to me?

Who are we to each other now that
there is no us, now that what we once

were is divided into me and you
who are not one but two separate and

unrelated persons except for that ex-
that goes in front of the words

that used to mean me, used to mean
you, words we rarely used (husband, wife)

as when we once posed (so young and helpless)
with our hands (yours, mine) clasped on the knife

that was sinking into the tall white cake.
All that sweetness, the layers of one thing

and then another, and then one thing again.

ALONE

Alone lets me listen closer
to the day, lets me hear
the wind between the leaves,
the dog barking across the marsh,
the clock ticking in the next room.

Nothing comes between me
and the wordless poem alone
is always making, the one
where birdsong rhymes with
tall grasses bending in the wind,

where leaf by leaf keeps time with
how the rain falls on the house,
where I am alone and could sing
this song that I am learning if only
I was made of perfect silence.

THE BOTTOM LINE

I make a map.
This is the edge of the world;
words end here, dreams too.

Then I make a chart.
This line shows the rise of expectations;
this might be called a crash.

I devise a secret code.
Nothing about it is obvious;
even I can't decipher it.

The recipe calls for telephones,
answering machines, and modems.
Fingers on the keyboard, silence.

When the bill comes it says:
broken hearts, parting lips, hands.
I pay for it all on time.

THE SOUND OF NO ONE CALLING

The sound of no one calling is a car
approaching and then heading into
the distance. It's the dishwasher
going through its cycles, one
click at a time, a squirrel chattering
in the tree outside the window.

The sound of no one calling is
empty shelves, the scrape of
the scoop at the bottom of the bin.
It's the faint light of the moon
through a cloudy veil, the ocean
inside a shell you hold up to your ear,
each time pretending to hear more.

It's rain on a tin roof—or a window
rattling in the wind, a needle drifting
aimlessly over the tractless vinyl
spinning on the turntable.
It's the furnace kicking in, the house
creaking, the clock, finally, ticking.

AISLE AND VIEW

Sometimes I was so lonely
that I liked grocery shopping.
I made it take a long time
and got every single thing
on the list. It wasn't important
to talk to anyone; I simply liked
the camaraderie of being
one body among others,
looking at the cake mixes.

I lingered in certain sections.
The spice aisle was educational,
and it always cheered me up
to read what the labels said.
There were commands: "Use
in barbecue sauce," "Rub
into steak prior to cooking,"
"Add zip to any salad," and
there were descriptions: "From
India, its earthy flavor is featured
in many Middle Eastern and
Latin American foods." I wished
I was from India and "earthy."

For hours (days, months, years!)
I wandered under the high
fluorescent lights. (Oh Philip Larkin!
What thoughts I had of you
among those sad shelves stacked
with cereal and sugar as white
as the lost light of distant stars!)

ONE AFTERNOON IN EARLY AUTUMN

One afternoon in early autumn, the wind
was in the treetops. In my mind's eye,
I saw bodies in bowler hats falling from

the sky, each one a bomb, ready
to open into umbrella. Vision
accompanied by engine sounds

and the usual whistle over
the clatter of iron wheels on track.
I swear, the sound of a train still

makes me lonely. Afternoon into
evening, and the wind tore leaves
(goldengrove unleaving?) from the

branches. I looked up into the star
domed sky through the maple
roof and saw it clear:

space was just a distance
between here and there; time
the thing between now and then,

and I was somewhere between
body and soul, broken-hearted
and riddled with light.

THE APOSTATE'S CREED

My fingers fumble on the keys;
I am caught between the pages.
In my dream I cut off my hair, then try
to put it back again. Life is crooked.

There is always one thing I need,
one thing missing, one thing I never
expected. Snow begins to fall and
falls all through the night. I wake, and

everything has been canceled. I love
the world when it is white, right after
the snow stops and the skies turn blue,
when there are no footprints.

Whatever is right was wrong once.
Do not say that this temple was built by
prayer or that church rose on a song;
there was blood, and gold changed hands.

EMPTY

I wanted so badly to be good.
I wanted everything to turn out right
in the end. I wanted to go to heaven.

Whatever I thought I should lose,
I lost; whatever the cost,
I paid it. Nothing was too much.

I worked hard at letting go; I
learned the art of denial. Wine
turned into water, bread to stone.

I was the bone singing in the desert,
the gate swinging on its hinge;
I was the bell ringing and ringing.

THE OLD ENMITY

His head was smaller than my thumb,
his tongue as thick as a piece of thread.

When I opened the door, I could look down
and see him gazing from under the doorframe.

His head was the size of a closed bud on
the maple tree, cherry-red, the color of bush

branches at the edge of the swamp. He flicked
his tongue in and out and coiled back as if

to strike, and so I worked out my fear with
a pointed stick, lifted him up and flung him

to the road, where he was quiet in the dust.
How I wished to crush him underfoot.

REASONS FOR LEAVING

Once I knew what brought
yellow and gold to the
green leaf: it was
an affectation of the light,
a slowing in the trunk and branch,
the broad cold hand of the sky,
needing, finally, to touch.

Now I think it is something in the stem,
a subtle severing at the base,
weakening where it joins the twig.
This happens when the river,
pulled up into the tree,
decides its had enough
of the sky,

or when the sun, so long
in secret synthesis with green,
turns its power down, abjuring
the alchemy of air and water.
Then the roots sigh and stop drinking
up the dark; the pulse in the trunk
dies away, and the leaves
can do nothing
but fall.

WHAT COMES AFTER

Repentance is not enough; forgiveness
is required, but you can only make a request,
then wait to see what happens. What you leave
at the doorstep, the letters that you send,
the many ways you try to repair the shame—
all of these things are better for the soul
than repentance, which is only one more
way of saying you would do it again.

When you ask to be forgiven, you must
not expect punishment without revenge;
there is no such thing as being even.
One day you may find that your offering
has been accepted, and the next day
you could be walking through the gate, almost
as if you were a prodigal coming
home to find that all has been forgiven.

ADVICE AND CONTENT

Pay attention to what you pay
attention to, or what—perhaps
as now—you do not give a fig for.

There are things that I would die
(and will, I suppose) to know; there
are things I will not sit still to learn.

When your mind wanders, wonder
what that means, meaning where is it
you visit instead of where you were

just then before you went astray?
Afterwards, when it's over, if ever
it is, think about how you started and

start to pick up pieces of yourself,
paying attention to each glittering shard,
remembering yourself into place.

IN THE WAKE

Everything I saved from the flood
went into the fire: one thing to keep
me warm, another because it
was old and useless, and one
just for the burning.

I had dreams, forgotten in the morning
as I dressed and got on with my life.
If I had it to do over again,
I would do nothing
the same.

Now that it's over, I don't know what
to make instead of a prayer. Now
the roof's gone, I can't
hear the sound of
the rain.

SEEING, UP CLOSE AGAIN

Like Gulliver in Brobdingnag, I
swooned to see again the immense
detail of the ordinary world:

the rippling surface of a fingernail,
exactly the color of a horn erupting
through the swirled-hair head of a calf,

the flayed landscape of skin where
catgut, pressing into the finger's
tip, made a ragged canyon,

the beaten sheen of a silver ring
around the pillared finger,
dark-tarnished runes

in its patterned crevices.
Nothing was too tiny for
my hungry eye,

nothing too finely etched.
I had grown weary of smooth
honed perfection, perceived from

a distance. Now, even the smallest
stroke of ink on paper was
deep enough to fold me in.

THE LAMP IN THE SPINE

How many words there were I did not know
then when I was beginning in the world,
when what was noted was not in books though
books there were, enough to comfort me, curled

up in some corner of the house, reading
under the covers with a light, intent
on the words sunk into the page, dreading
the moment when that unmapped continent

would blur and disappear and leave me lost
with only the sense of having traveled
far and in the company of a ghost
whose voice wound inside me and unraveled

the singular fabric of my being,
the flat canvas of my practiced seeing.

CAFÉ SONG

The shadow in the window reaches up.
Outside, in the street, a body disappears.
These voices that I hear are falling to
pieces, dishes rattle on the table,
and heavy rain begins to fall over
the endless stretch of headlights.
You look up, hundreds of miles away.

A new song begins, and everyone
moves to its beat, as though stepping
onto a moving train, standing
in bright sunshine for the first
time in days. It slips, falls into
a voice fretting the pavement like
the flickering dash of the white line.

From the other side of the room
I seem to be a woman bent
over a map, stirring the ashes
of a dying fire, taking down the
thoughts of trees, leaf by leaf. I
look up and greet whatever gaze
meets mine, returning to the song.

RIDING ON FAITH

I asked myself, "What is like the sound
of chairs being moved into place
in a room beneath where you
are lying on a narrow bed
covered with white chenille?"

I asked, "What is like the heaviness
in one eye as you try to bring
the world back into focus? Where
is the lever that will lift
that curtain? What wind will
carry the clouds away?"

When I remembered how I had
come across the fields at midday,
navigating by the blue blur of signs,
I asked myself, "What is like
Providence? What won't we do
to have the waters parted before us?"

THIS BODY

When I stepped ashore in this body
I was recognized at once
and given a name.

My bones were smaller, but the shape
of the cheek and the chin
are the same.

This is the only body I know: this color
my eyes, this color my skin.
Every scar is mine.

I have become as tall, as slim, as old
as I am. My voice has carried the weight
of what I had to say,

Words were scattered along the way: words
on gravel roads, in hallways and staircases.
Words on a wire.

Somewhere in a field, my hair. Somewhere in a lake,
my skin, some rooftop where my gaze rested,
some star, a wish.

This is my address on earth: temporary, fragile,
a name in the phone book,
at the moment alive.

BEGINNING AGAIN

When I begin, it is difficult
to say what I have been waiting for,
or why at the moment, there is nothing
on this page.
          Don't try so hard
I tell myself. Anyone, moving through
the same long days, in a body
weary as yours, would—as you do
now—find comfort in the sun
and the sound of the wind as
it takes away the deep drifts
of winter snow.
          Now that you have
this hour to yourself, you might
consider what will never happen again
and how you let it go without
a word. Now you might consider
how the words you found will never
take the place of what was not
happening around you.

WHAT THE ELDERS TAUGHT US

Thinking about something does not make it
happen. I was thinking about calling
you, but I didn't; I was hoping that you
would call me, but the phone never rang. Once

I had the power to will things into
being. I would dream about you and you
would appear from thousands of miles away.
We answered each other before we called.

No one would believe how we were back then.
What I liked especially was the way old
people smiled at us even though they knew
our fortune was not to be together.

They liked the way we accepted our fate;
they knew how heaven sometimes comes too late.

THE FUTURE ARCHAIC

I will wish that we were back then
in what is now what someday was
going to be. You will remember
what we did this day as something
we could write out in a story,
something from long before our times.
When we think of back now then, we
will wish that we were here again.

You will say that I have forgot
the future, that the past is not
going to happen anymore.
All the while the hours will roll
on, like boxcars across the land,
the minutes shining in the sun.

WALKING IN EARLY JUNE

Mornings, we walk down the hill, past houses
where someone's been painting, and someone else
has been adding a garage. The day
lilies open wide their tiger mouths; rust
edges the big heads of the peonies.

We detour through the Post Office garden,
reading, as we walk, the gold letters on
the white brick wall: "Bare night is best.
Bare earth ...." We loop through the hosta, past
the tall vases, reading

       "where the voice that
is great within us rises up...." Then we
are out on the sidewalk again, our eyes
now on the lake, where a few sailboats skim
the flat blue. We cross and walk along

railroad tracks to the old depot, passing
shrubs and roses to the dock. Our feet
on the boards make a wooden echo
beneath us as we walk straight out over
the water: gulls wheeling, the sun rising.

SOUNDINGS

In the afternoon of summer, sounds
come through the window: a tractor
muttering to itself as it

pivots at the corner of the
hay field, stalled for a moment
as the green row feeds into the baler.

The wind slips a whisper behind
an ear; the noise of the highway
is like the dark green stem of a rose.

From the kitchen the blunt banging
of cupboard doors and wooden chairs
makes a lonely echo in the floor.

Somewhere, between the breeze
and the faraway sound of a train,
comes a line of birdsong, lightly
threading the heavy cloth of dream.

IN THE MIDDLE OF THINGS

At the gate, waiting for the arrival
of whoever has gone away and now
is coming back or whoever now is
only leaving and perhaps may never
return, I notice how time has spent each
face a little, rubbing shadows on the
cheeks that lean against the darkened plate of
glass, carving lines under the eye as night
continues long and the distances do not
go away. I notice that we are not
as young as I remember us in a time
that only now has begun to happen.
I should remember this all backwards so
it will make sense to us when we get there.

AFTER, ALWAYS AFTER

I wake up wondering which side of things
I'm on. Is it before or after now?
After. It will always be after, though
the world outside my window is green,
and light floods the horizon to fill up
the bowl of the sky. I check the voices
on the radio: they're sunny, partly
cloudy at news time. Traffic is moving
on the roads and in the air; I hear it
in the usual places. Last night I dreamed
it never happened, that the past was not
yet passed, and there was still a chance this day
was on its way to a different time
where before and after were words that rhymed.

NOW THAT ANYTHING COULD HAPPEN

You now know that anything could happen;
things that never happened before, things that
only happened in movies and nightmares
are happening now, as if nothing could
stop them. You know now that you are not safe,
you know you live in fragile skin and bones,
that even steel and concrete can melt away,
and that the earth itself can come unhinged,
shaken from its orbit around the sun.
You know, now that anything can happen,
it's hard to know what will, and what will you
do now that you know? What words will you say
now that you could say anything? What hands
will you hold? Whose heart will beat inside you?

LEAVING FRIDAY HARBOUR

This is the melody for a movie
that I might make one day. Everything
could happen within its lilting measures:

the day she met him along the boardwalk,
the way the sailboats were slowly leaving
the harbor, the way the sun was setting.

Or this could be a wedding song, something
you'd play at the very end, when the crowd
is waving as the couple glides away,

or this could be your funeral music—
why not be sweetly borne on the journey,
why not have everyone's heart on your way?

Or this could be the song of paradise:
the first thing you hear on the other side.

WHAT TO PACK

Either nothing you've ever worn before
or everything old and warm. Only
one of anything, but bring along all

of something. Don't forget a few worthless
items so you can leave what you really
need at home. Pack lightly and pack often;

practice packing in the middle of night.
Before you fall asleep, picture the trip
you have always wanted to take and pack

the things you'll need there: a lute, a pear tree,
and a dove the color of a cloud packed
with thousands of raindrops, each one of them

standing at the open door in the sky
with a ticket and a tiny suitcase.

GETTING THE MACHINE

It was good to hear
my own voice again
when I called, after
being gone for weeks.
I sounded about the same.
I hadn't changed my name;
didn't have a foreign accent.
I just said I couldn't
come to the phone right then,
exactly the way I'd been
saying it for years,
and so I left myself
a little message
saying how sorry
I was I wasn't there,
and that I'd be
home soon. I tried to
think of what I'd want
to hear myself saying
and say it right.

SOME GLAD MORNING

One day, something very old
happened again. The green
came back to the branches,
settling like leafy birds
on the highest twigs;
the ground broke open
as dark as coffee beans.

The clouds took up their
positions in the deep stadium
of the sky, gloving the
bright orb of the sun
before they pitched it
over the horizon.

It was as good as ever:
the air was filled
with the scent of lilacs
and cherry blossoms
sounded their long
whistle down the track.
It was some glad morning.

AT THE MOMENT

Suddenly, I stopped thinking about Love,
after so many years of only that,
after thinking that nothing else mattered.

And what was I thinking of when I stopped
thinking about Love? Death, of course—what else
could take Love's place? What else could hold such force?

I thought about how far away Death once
had seemed, how unexpected that it could
happen to someone that I knew quite well,

how impossible that this should be the
normal thing, as natural as frost and
winter. I thought about the way we'd aged,

how skin fell into wrinkles, how eyes grew
dim; then (of course) my love, I thought of you.

NOW, FINALLY, A LOVE SONG

Now, finally, I'll write you a love song,
or, at least, something that we're both
in, saying things that I should have said long
ago, and you'll be happy to hear them.

Now finally, I'll say what a wonder
you are, and you'll wonder why I never
told you that before, and I'll ask whether
we could make a life together under

the circumstances, which seem to have changed
since yesterday and everyday since
we met each other long ago, distance
hard to measure, two lives rearranged.

And finally, I know what we should do:
I know the song; I'll sing it to you.

JOYCE SUTPHEN is the author of *Straight Out of View*, winner of the 1994 Barnard New Women Poets Prize, and *Coming Back to the Body* (2000). She has won many awards, including a Loft-McKnight Award, the Eunice Tietjen's Memorial Award (Poetry), a Minnesota State Arts Board Fellowship, a Salzburg Fellowship, and Travel and Study awards from the Jerome Foundation. Currently Associate Professor of English at Gustavus Adolphus College in St. Peter, Minnesota, she holds degrees in creative writing and Shakespeare from the University of Minnesota.

ACKNOWLEDGMENTS

I would like to thank the Anderson Center (Red Wing, Minnesota) and the Writer's House (Knockeven, County Clare, Ireland) for residencies during the time when some of these poems were written. I am also grateful to the Minnesota State Arts Board, the McKnight Foundation, The Loft, and Gustavus Adolphus College for their generous support.

GRATEFUL ACKNOWLEDGMENT is made to the following journals where some of these poems were first published:

"Naming the Stars," *Poetry*, July 2000.
"Raku Songs," *Gettysburg Review*, Fall 2001.
"Gone Missing," *Water~Stone Review*, Fall 2002.
"To Take Her Home," *Gettysburg Review*, Fall 2001.
"How We Ended Up Together," *North Stone Review*, Spring 2002.
"Learning By Heart," *Poetry*, July 2000.
"The Problem Was," *Poetry*, February 2000.
"Handprint," Losing Touch," "Since You Will Not Send Me Word," *Three Candles*, Summer 2002.
"Crossing the Seine at Pont Neuf," *Peregrine*, Fall 2001.
"Hanging Up," *North Stone Review*, Spring 2002.
"Polaroid #2," *Northeast Review*, Winter 2003.
"Measuring the Distance," "The Bottom Line," "Advice and Content," "The Old Enmity," "Café Song" *North Stone Review*, Spring 2003.
"Notice," *Poetry*, February 2002.
"Ever After," *Poetry*, February 2003.
"Alone," *Gettysburg Review*, Fall 2001.
"The Sound of No One Calling," *Northeast Review*, Winter 2003.
"One Afternoon in Early Autumn," *Loonfeather*, Summer 1999.
"The Apostate's Creed," *Hayden's Ferry Review*, Spring/Summer 2000.
"Empty," *Sidewalks*, Summer 2001.
"In the Wake," *The Vincent Brothers Review*, Issue # 20.
"Seeing, Up Close Again," *Caffeine Destiny*, Fall 2001.
"This Body," *Poetry*, January 2001.
"Beginning Again," *Water~Stone*, Fall 2001.
"What the Elders Taught Us," *North Stone Review*, Spring 2002.
"Soundings" *Sidewalks*, Summer 2001.
"In the Middle of Things," *A View from the Loft*, October 2001.
"After, Always, After," *Pieta*, Spring 2002.
"Now that Anything Can Happen," *A View from the Loft*, October 2001.
"At the Moment," *Great River Review*, Spring-Summer 2003.

CPSIA information can be obtained
at www.ICGtesting.com
Printed in the USA
JSHW080751150723
44537JS00002B/1